STRAUNGE WUNDER

~ OR ~

THE
METALIRIOUS PLEASURES
OF
NEURALCHEMY

STRAUNGE WUNDER

~ OR ~

THE

METALIRIOUS PLEASURES

OF

NEURALCHEMY

....

BY

STEVE VENRIGHT

ILLUSTRATED BY

RICHARD KIRK

....

TORTOISESHELL & BLACK · TORONTO

CANADIAN CATALOGUING IN PUBLICATION DATA

Venright, Steve, 1961–
    Straunge Wunder

Poems.

ISBN 1-896901-00-X

I. Title. II. The metalirious pleasures of neuralchemy.

PS8593.E58S73   1996   C811'.54   C96-931944-4
PR9199.3.V48S73 1996

TORTOISESHELL & BLACK
7 Walmer Rd. #707
Toronto, Ontario
M5R 2W8

I utter myself by seeing.

PAUL FOSTER CASE
The Book of Tokens

for

Dale, Jesse, and Kerry

. . . and in memory of the
several million starfish
who died mysteriously
along the shores of the
Arctic White Sea in May
of 1990.

TABLE OF CONTENTS

The Contented Hour

Now is the contented hour of postwar sonic morphine and drunken cheerleaders collapsed on fireside rugs beneath fragrant blankets of pipesmoke.

Now is the contented hour of scrapfed kittens purring on patriarchal laps stained with newsprint and rifle oil.

Now is the contented hour filled with the lullaby of backfiring cars and the muffled clangour of rinsing dishes.

Now is the contented hour when succulent jealous ruminations flit beneath slanting toupées like deluded moths under opaque lampshades.

Idle libidinal voodoo in the cataleptic armchair of remorse. A silent righteous discourse sucked mindlessly away like doghair into the squealing vacuum.

SICK STORIES

A basket of tangerines falling from a height of six storeys. Shadows of cormorants on the pavement below. Shingles detach themselves from the roof and flutter up like playing cards from the deck of a spastic gambler. I take my time-lapse capsules and watch the boatrace from an unfinished bridge. Tortoiseshell cats lick my ankles.

Houses of Skin

O membranous circuitry, wield aloft the glistening viscera of this turbulescent grace. A state so refined and empowered it cannot be transposed, or so stupid and glorious it cannot be conveyed.

A holographic fountain at which we drink unfulfilled day and night as the torrential rains liberate us from these soluble temples of flesh, these houses of skin.

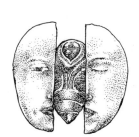

THUNDERHEADS — *for Baudelaire*

"Tell me, enigmatic stranger — what brand of thunder do you favour?"

"Why, I like DISTANT METALLIC CASCADE™ — satisfyingly voluptuous, but never overpowering in its remote grandeur. And you, odd inquisitor — what style of atmosphonic gets you off?"

"Well, my fellow global village idiot, IMPERIAL SKYCRUNCHER™ is the one that blasts *my* dendrites. With its delectable stentorian crepitations of pure synesthetic manna, who could resist the pontifical marvels of this convulsive aural leviathan!"

And with that the two strangers parted, their lightning rods swaying like the masts of stormtossed whaling ships in a wild Melvillean ocean.

I Am Still Unflayed

Well, they've done it again. They've locked up a man who looks like a devil and they're tearing off pieces of his skin and selling them as souvenirs. But you won't read about that in the newspaper – no, you'll read about the woman who planted her flowerbed in the shape of a moose she and her husband ran over by mistake in their car, you'll read about a strike at the pet shop and the scabs who broke the picket line shielding themselves with squirrel monkeys, or you'll read about a new design for the flag – but you won't read about that. It's the sort of thing that happens all the time, though, and I thought you should know about it. There's no skin off my back but one day they'll catch me too because I look like a goddamn demon right now and there's no way of telling.

I hide in my tent watching UFOs through the screen, and if the church or the cops don't nab me I bet those buggers up there in their saucers will. I set my traps and hop a morning freight for the office – I'm an architect by profession, that's the irony. For lunch I plunk a ferret in the microwave, dine, then strip and splash myself down at the water cooler before everyone gets back from their break. They all think I'm so dedicated because I never go out, but really I'm just cautious. I always get a nosebleed just before quitting time, and when I bleed I get spasms too, so the stuff goes all over the damn place. That's when they call on Moe the janitor to take me down to the boiler room, where I won't stain any blueprints. It's Moe who tells me about all the recent flayings and where to get skin cheap if I want it and about the time he knocked up a goat and sold the kid to some cult that masquerades as a circus. When I congeal enough to sit up straight we open my lunchbox and take out the ferret guts I've saved. Moe lays them out on the workbench and does the augury for the day, looking like an auditor going over financial statements. So far he has correctly predicted one space shuttle explosion (the second one), four earthquakes, the outcome of three consecutive curling championships, a hernia (his own), and the rise of fascism in Canada. He's been wrong a lot more times than he's been right, but it's a hobby and a good one. Some people like to play chess, some do crossword puzzles, others like to go out to the theatre – Moe tells the future by staring at my leftovers, and there's no harm done. When it's finished he wraps up the guts in the Page 3 pin-up of the local rag and tosses them in the incinerator. Then he lets me out through the back, gives me a kiss on the cheek, and sends me off to wait for the next freight home.

BORDER DISSOLUTION

The guy at the customs booth on the American side of the bridge asked us where we lived.

"Turrawna," we chimed proudly.

"What is the purpose of your visit?" he inquired.

"We're just comin' over to shoot a few people then going right back," I replied.

"Are you bringing over any citrus fruit or pornographic literature?"

"No sir, we just have some raw beets and a copy of the *Surrealist Manifesto*."

He jutted his crocodilian head a little closer and I halted my reflex to close the window using the automatic button.

"Is that the *First* or *Second* manifesto?" he demanded.

"The *First*," I lied, remembering the ideological recisions Aragon and Sadoul were forced to make when Communist Party officials objected to aspects of the *Second Manifesto* during their visit to Moscow.

This seemed to satisfy our sombre reptilian interrogator, but it was evident he had at least one more good question for us.

"Do either of you have any MDMA or other mood-altering substances in your possession?"

"No, indeed," asserted my companion.

"Thanks anyway – feeling kinda shitty today," he confided. "Okay, you folks have a nice visit."

"Don't you want to check our trunk?" I offered.

"No, not right now."

At last we were on our way again to the symposium on consciousness and the brain. We weren't really going to shoot anyone, of course, but felt it best to conceal the true nature of our visit. Even a former president and his wife thought it was okay to have a brain — in fact they dedicated a whole decade to the thing. But the subject of consciousness, we knew, was another matter entirely.

Instructions for Disposal

I read this book in which the author, a Dr Tetrau-Porren, claims that over two hundred people are buried alive each day in the United States of America. I find that to be a rather conservative estimate.

As for me, when I go, I want them to wait at least a week before they put me under. I had a friend — they buried her, and two days later she was back at work. Showed up at the office covered in filth, embalmed and wearing false eyelashes. Buried her with her cellular phone, so when she came to she called the office manager from her coffin. He came and dug her up, gave her coffee and donuts, brought her in and set her down at the terminal, and away she went, fast as ever. Said she wasn't scared — hadn't donated any organs or anything. She was just glad to be back at work and have the whole thing behind her.

But me, when I go, if you want to mince me, go ahead. Toss me to the sharks. You want to get out your blowtorches, be my guest. Spare me the resurrection. I'm gone, I'm gone.

Straunge Wunder

My last incarnation lasted only a few hours. I was born cyclopean with both penis and vagina, a long tapir-esque snout, and wings instead of arms. There were two legs, granted, but one to the fore and one to the aft. Also present was a majestic prehensile tail loping downward from the shoulder blades, which I'm sure could have been put to good use if not for the brevity of its animation.

The midwife tried to hide me, more for her own protection than mine, I suspect, but to no avail. My mother, dead from horror at the sight of me, was little comfort to my father as he lay expiring in a bloody fashion from projectile wounds inflicted by his morally superior neighbours. It was a couple hundred years ago in the south of England, and births like the one I had committed were not yet commonplace.

As for me, I outlived them all (my midwife having been fatally ravished by samaritans from the clergy), rising on my nimble fleshy wings to empty my labyrinthine bowels upon the righteous throng below. Having eluded flying rocks and slashing scythes, I met my end, ironically, in a freak accident: a head-on collision with a rare diurnal bat of monstrous proportion (was I immune to sonar?) snuffed the brief but glorious flame of my existence.

If you go to a large metropolitan library housing an extensive collection of periodicals on microfilm, you can read for yourself the commendably unbiased account of my life in the *Gentleman's Magazine*, March 1739; or you can take my word for it – I am a lawyer now and, as such, pledged to truth.

omnino res videre probus

IN ALL THINGS SEE THE GOOD

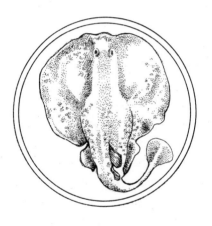

Thank You for Not Chasing Your Tail

The birds were clanging in the trees. They tasted much like the motor of an overworked electric fan doused with absinthe. For once, "eating the air" seemed less a fanciful Symbolist aspiration than a metabolic necessity. Shrubberies cringed like melting cellophane at my approach, resuming their topiary propriety in my passing. Even the sound of my own voice, taunting me from across the road, was not enough to distract me from my happiness.

Lucid Dreaming Reality Test

In order to become adept at lucid dreaming it is recommended that you perform simple tests intermittently throughout the day as a means of determining that you are really awake. Such exercises, if repeated frequently enough, will carry over into your true dreaming state so that the likelihood of becoming conscious of your oneiric condition will be increased.

The following reality checks are provided as examples of this method:

1. Telephone any branch of the Federal Government. If your call is answered, you are probably dreaming. If it is answered by someone other than an alleged government employee – a museum curator, perhaps, or a hair salon receptionist – check the number and dial again.

2. Stare fixedly at the person nearest you, then turn away for a moment. If during this interval the person has transformed into, let's say, a batfaced magistrate (assuming he or she wasn't already such), you are almost surely asleep.

3. Remove your clothes in a public place and assess the reactions of those around you. Until you have performed this action *while definitely awake* you will not be able to distinguish between the responses of material witnesses and those of dream characters. When in doubt, repeat suggestion #1.

4. Invite a member of the preferred gender to engage in intimate acts with you. If you are dreaming, a glorious realm of sensual fulfilments will be yours to explore (most lucid dreamers describe their somnolent sexual encounters as their most intense and satisfying). If you are not dreaming, you might at least get lucky now and again. Of course this proposal could have awkward consequences, so it is wise to carry a LUCID DREAMER REALITY TEST card to present in the event that offence is taken by a three-dimensional subject of your experimentation. NOTE: *Perceived possession of this card does not necessarily mean that you are experiencing external reality.*

The practice of these and similar tests of your own invention is sure to provide you with initiation into the fantastical realm of lucid dreaming. Therein you will find the greatest sense of liberation and the truest expression of free will.

Many are they who go through their waking lives unconscious, but few are they with the gift of being conscious while asleep.

JAR

Some kids on the sidewalk near a vacant lot have captured something in a glass jar and are ogling it with mischievous delight.

"You better poke some holes in the lid so it can breathe," I suggest as I near them, remembering all the tiny suffocations of my own childhood.

They look at me as if I'm completely crazy. Peering closer I see that there's a human tongue inside the jar.

Embarrassed by my absurd suggestion I continue on my way.

❀

Aeroray

At times like this I become an aeronautic manta ray gliding down the murky luminescent hallways of your silent violet sanctuary. One word and I will burst into flames, to rise from my powdery ashes like a stray aquatic phoenix.

The neighbours can think what they like when they see me float through your open window, rise above the telephone wires, and disappear.

One Night in Iceland

Water gushes from the mouth of a fish cradled in the mermaid's arms. I drape my yellow raincoat over her shoulders of stone and place my scurvied lips upon her cold green neck.

Vapocetaceaglaciogenesis

1. We pull flesh from the clouds, enwrap ourselves and descend. No one else is here yet. The oceans are all empty. We become as big as our want.

2. The spindrift exemplifies our thoughts and longings. The ocean on which it skims is, so to speak, God. It's remarkable how close the whales get to our faces before we detect them — and this in water so clear you can't perceive it.

3. Omission contours of erasing glaciers. Frozen colour photographs anachronous amid monochromes. Subject matter: the Martian Sphinx and the Glastonbury Zodiac superimposed.

Tiny Satellites

There's a kind of moss on the old tiles which eats right out of your hand. There are black shiny feathers falling all the time and you can see faces and pictures when you look at them, scenes of strange and beautiful lands. The fish fly already poached out of the geysers and land in your lap. Tiny satellites float around your head and send images to – I don't know – other planets, I guess.

FIELD NOTE

I would come out of trance at the end of each session in a state of sublime sensory acuteness and with extraordinary animal magnetism. This mesmerically acquired ability proved useful in hunting, an activity I would normally disdain. Large mutant rodents and small hybrid mammals emerging from the thicket would be drawn to my person, sometimes twirling rump over snout through the air till they clung like living fridge magnets posting their own death sentences to my body. The hungry botanists would then stumble forth, surround me, and – depending on how badly I was being bitten – either strangle or crush or stab the poor bastards till, demagnetized, they dropped dead at my feet.

Reincarceration

I can only tell you what I know. I am a nine-year-old Zolguvian girl enslaved inside a treehouse made of transparent acrylic melted over a toothpick frame. My captors bring me salty ice cream sticks flavoured with anise and pomegranate. They ask nothing of me and promise my release upon the reincarnation of Wilhelm Reich, which they mistakenly insist will coincide with the discovery of an underwater city based on the Golden Section. I have not yet managed to convince them that I am him.

In Aisle Eight

You march through my temples at dusk with your flatulent weimaraners and your wagons of cooling magma. I'll stand in these aisles forever, trying on makeup, my mind not fully assimilated by this scaffolding of guts.

All He was Worth

He left a note tied to a bone, smashed all the billiard balls, unwired the doorbell. He piled all the empty breadbags in a neat stack and set fire to them. He left a message on his doctor's answering machine requesting that all his medical records be sent to a cubist veterinarian located in a trailer park near the quarry. He defrosted the fridge. He drew a line from Point A to Point B, bisected it, then erased the unwanted portion. He fed the cat (to the dog). Then he lost consciousness, but so briefly he was not even aware it had happened. The next moment he was beside himself with glee, then a little to the rear feeling mildly dismayed, before losing sight of himself completely over by the radiator. In that instant half his life flashed before his eyes – the half which hadn't happened yet – and since it looked pretty good he decided to give it a whirl. With destiny spread out before him, like the unclad polystyrene legs of a toppled storefront mannequin truncated at the belly, he strode confidently up to the door and knocked loudly. He paused and rapped again, but there was no one outside. With the same sense of guilt and expectation with which he'd been born, he opened the door a crack and peered out. On the billboard across the street he saw a picture of himself leaning on a giant can opener beneath the slogan YE ARE GODS. He ripped the door from its hinges, hurled himself down the concrete steps, and ran through the world with his arms outstretched in joy, screaming for all he was worth.

An Introduction to
Your New TVI Septal Electrode

Congratulations on choosing TORPOR VIGIL INDUSTRIES, the world's finest purveyor of septal electrodes (sales and implantation) since 1691.

The model with which you have been fitted includes a remote control, allowing friends or loved ones to transmit euphoriagrams from any location within a three kilometre radius. There's a synesthesia adaptor for multi-sensory stimulation, as well as an optional audio input that's pitch and timbre sensitive. When not in use, this unit produces an automatic 7.83Hz Schumann frequency so that you can resonate perpetually with the Earth's ionosphere cavity. Guarantee extends throughout the apocalypse and covers improbable malfunctions due to sunstorm interference (not valid in the event of polar shift or during periods of officially issued Magnetosphere Mutation Warnings).

The TVI Septal Electrode – a sensible alternative to addictive substances and mundane or immoral entertainments.

Excerpts from the forthcoming DREAM
DICTIONARY OF CARVOLIUS,
*as dictated by the Carvolian Himself
through the instrument S.Venright —
presented by Thee Numinous Ordur uv
Carvolian Aspirants*

Thee Numinous Ordur uv Carvolian Aspirants is
a registered cult (lic.#612788) devoted tu thee
insemignosis uv fertile cognitive instruments prepared
tu receive thee Majycke Trancemissions uv Carvolius,
"Knight of the Living Dead" & "Disembodied Orator
of Revelation" (the KOLD DOOR). Tu becum an initiate
& achoir a copy uv our colouring book send a urine
sample (anybody's) & £23 tu thee address below, or
fax us a xerox of your genitals inscribed with your
bank account number (yes, your genitals, not the
xerox — it's an inlodge means of identification, as
ordained by the Carvolian).

THEE NUMINOUS ORDER UV CARVOLIAN ASPIRANTS, INC.
Attn: Noah Veil, Arch-Shepherd
         (Membership Drive Committee)
Cattlebong Farm, 23 Spilyerguts Road,
The Squeeblies, Fritterwig-Upon-Kunnit
Ultimagog, Somerset UB12 4PP
tel: 327-968-9288
fax: 327-169-1961

The Dream Dictionary of Carvolius — *selected entries*

BESTIALITY ✳ Dreaming of sexual coupling with an animal betrays an unwholesome fixation with members of the animal kingdom. Excepted are cases in which a woman dreams of sexual intercourse with a swan (*see* MYTHOLOGY) or a man dreams of sexual intercourse with a shark (*see* LATENT SURREALIST TENDENCIES AND MALDORORIAN COMPLEXES MANIFESTING IN TESTOSTERONE-CHARGED DREAM SITUATIONS). However, for a sleeper of either sex to dream of such things as humping a mudpuppy or being shagged by a groundsloth, the significance is clear: immediate psychiatric attention should be sought upon waking.

BUTCHER ✳ *Being a butcher yourself.* To be a butcher in your dream suggests that you ate something odd before going to bed. If you are a butcher by profession, you probably did eat something odd before going to bed. ✳ *Someone else is a butcher.* To see someone performing the functions of a butcher or wearing the garb of a butcher in your dream implies that you feel others are being unjustly critical of your actions and personality. Try not to be such a deplorable twerp and see if you can do something useful in your life for a change. ✳ *Neither you nor anyone else is a butcher.* If you have a dream in which no one is a butcher, the likelihood of success in your current business endeavours is very slim. This can be rectified by thinking about butchers all day until eventually one appears in a dream (or by eating something rank and peculiar at bedtime).

CIGAR (see PENIS) ✳ A cigar in a dream is merely a cigar.

LEMUR HEWN SEAJET ✳ To perceive in your sleep the image of a small Malagasy primate sculpting an aerodynamic vessel with which to fly over a body of water is truly to be the honoured victim of a visionary pun. What you are really observing is a symbolically transposed revelation of the marriage between Heaven and Earth, the kingdom beyond apocalypse, the next dimension of divine human habitation. To confirm this, one need merely condense the dream's content to its simplest written form – LEMUR HEWN SEAJET – then rearrange the letters till their most sensible anagrammatic structure emerges. In doing so you are building in words what the dream suggests you long to build spiritually: THE NEW JERUSALEM.

LICORICE ✳ Licorice dreams are generally auspicious. To find yourself eating licorice in a telephone booth while an Amazonian shaman in a bowler hat waits outside usually means that you will receive by mail a special introductory offer from a health club franchise. If you are an Amazonian shaman you will already know this.

PRECOGNITION ✳ To dream of something that has not yet happened means there is a particular event in your life that is still to come to pass. Pay special attention to the content of this dream for clues as to the nature of this event. Because sequential time is an illusion sustained by consciousness for its own convenience (*e.g.* for the sake of commerce, sports, etc.), one may also dream of things that have already happened.

RAT CHOCOLATE ✳ To dream of rats lapping chocolate is a sign that your pancreas trouble will improve. If one or more of the rats is piebald you are certain to receive adequate remuneration for malpractice related – or perhaps unrelated – to this ailment. NOTE: *Rats lapping shit is a different kettle of fish altogether (see* COPRODENTIA).

TOOTHLESS NUDITY ✳ To dream that your teeth are falling out as you stand naked in a schoolyard doesn't mean anything, really – its just one of those sketchily mnemonic situational configurations resulting from haphazard neuronal firings with which the REM state is wont to beleaguer you now and again. Disregard any references to such content you may have read in other dream dictionaries, most of which are complete bullshit.

LAGAMORPHOGENESIS

Dangerous gong. A tubular morphogenetic drone. You mustn't conceive within three days of hearing it or your offspring will be tremendous, they'll be hilarious. Critters you could not imagine except maybe in your most hyperlucid dopamine-flooded dreams.

Speaking of which, I know a nifty way of objectifying dream images. It's done with lasers, sonic beat frequencies, and pulsed scalar field generators aligned to produce interference patterns. The concept of *neuronal ricochet* is involved, and the dreamer has to be skilled at simultaneously stabilizing oneiric impressions and communicating with external technicians conducting the procedure.

We got it to work once so far, materialized a sort of globular lagamorph – a droopy Mayanesque rabbit which lived for a few days, without eating or making a sound, then appeared to melt away into nothingness. Strange that we should mimic a magician's trick in our first successful experiment. Stranger still that the person who dreamt the beast into existence was completely unable, when awake, to perceive its objectified three-dimensional form (though our descriptions confirmed that it was indeed the creature of his dream).

Vacancies

Enters like a thin pyrite disc through a mail slot, its fur oiled and glowing. From behind the crumbling tiles emerge blind translucent salamanders, frictionless and unseen even as they grapple up the slippery thighs of showering houseguests. Miniature vermiform picto- grams beneath the devastated veranda. Videotaped assassinations in the lounge.

OPERATION:RAPTURE

Then they sacrificed the control specimens and established a rococo nerve lattice among the surviving patients in quarantine at the Involute Gear Company Wholesale Warehouse Clearance Centre Plaza subterfuge zone headquarters while we interrogated moribund corpus callosum severance victims unwittingly housing parasitic download fragments from hollow earth abductee myth-virus experimental subjects being used for bioseduction of trance-channeled ectovapour personas generated by noötropically injected mediums entrained to a theta beat-frequency pulsed neuroelectrically and cyberphotically until spontaneous induction of pathological visionary states delivered them unto a religio-erotic delirium not unlike that suffered by witnesses of the geopathically manifested BVM hallucination orgy seen on the briefing film screened just prior to the outset of OPERATION:RAPTURE. Meanwhile the same special-effects crew responsible for filming the hoaxed Mars landing catastrophe produced footage allegedly shot on location at the multiple witness mesa crash site, but the craft depicted was of military antigravitational origin and the bodies were strictly second-generation earthborn hybrid clone failures dressed in surplus spacemonkey suits manufactured for the aborted PROJECT:VIMANA missions. Diversionary tornadoes aimed at blackout centres receiving ELF waves to stimulate excessive noradrenal secretion and induce violent pandemonium in the populace were subject to unanticipated trajectory repulsions and went astray like golfballs slicing into adjacent fairways. The satellite assassinations, on the other hand, were executed with precision and – despite the total corporeal incineration peculiar to spontaneous human combustion – the media has accepted unquestioningly the pronouncements of mundane causes fabricated by bribed medical investigators made compliant by threat of similar remote annihilation. Thanks to new evidence widely propagated by our Historical Clarifications Department, recent polls show that suicide is now commonly accepted as the cause of death in the J.F.K. incident. Revelations are also forthcoming regarding an alleged crucifixion that has been in the news for a couple of millennia. A verdict of accidental death is expected to resolve any confusion that may have arisen as a result of this case.

Jesus Christ Meets the Queen of England in the Presence of a Sinner

They told me where Jesus was hanging so I went over to check it out. The Queen was there, on her own, looking meagrely interested as though inspecting an exhibit of fossilized dung presented in her honour. She acted like she didn't want to be recognized, standing perfectly still, hoping I wouldn't notice her, but there she was in her gloves and glittercap, and there was nobody else around. Nobody except Jesus of course, and the two spider monkeys on either side of him, each with a spike through its head and drooping like a hairy marionette on its wooden pole.

Jesus himself was asleep, his head slung down and his mouth gaping, manifesting a superhuman pool of drool on the ruddy earth below. He was dreaming, and you could tell that if his hands and feet weren't nailed so tight they'd be twitching like the eager paws of a somnolent puppy. Instead his fingers simply fluttered spasmodically, as if he were playing a huge hyperspatial bandoneon. And so I thought of the *nuevo tango* of Astor Piazzolla, and it was this music – so lilting, lyrical, delirious, orgasmic, and lugubrious – which filled the scene for me (sometimes I can imagine things so vividly it seems they're really happening).

Then Jesus awoke with a huge snort, followed immediately by a yelp of intense pain. Next he tried like hell to get off the cross, but he was like a mouse caught in a sticky-trap, or a tigermoth with its wings fried to an outhouse lightbulb, or a fighting hockey player torn away from the scrum by two linesmen but still struggling fiercely to get in a few punches.

As soon as he noticed the Queen and me, he froze — eyes wide, quivering lips agape, a supremely sheepish look blushing across his divine countenance. The Queen farted delicately in surprise, began to address the Messiah, then thought better of it and looked down with embarrassment to the two oriental massage balls she seemed to be bearing as a gift. I turned my head, automatically pretending I'd been looking somewhere else, then with unanticipated grace assumed a worshipful kneeling position.

This seemed to bring the poor fellow back to his senses, for he began to utter theosophical snippets in a tone of stumbling majesty and gothic luminescence. The image of a cracked stained glass window melting in a churchfire came to mind. As he spoke he looked directly into our eyes, from the Queen to me and back again — really entering into his element, a man in full control of his pain, though, sadly, not his mind.

I say unto thee: Whomsoever shalt leave his cake out in the rain, so shalt he be pressed in love's hot fevered iron like a stripèd pair of pants. And be alarmèd not if thou hearest a bustle in thy hedgerow, for it is but the May Queen bringing thee tea and oranges in the windmills of thy mind. Thou shalt not sleep in the subway nor shalt thou stand in the pouring rain, for the door of the Lord is always open and His path is free to walk. Be thou not shackled by forgotten words and bonds, and know ye that the world will not be cursing or forgiving. Yea though the wheat-fields and the clotheslines and the highways come between us, in silence might I runneth still; tears of joy might staineth my face; and the sum-mer sun might burneth me till I'm blind; but not to where I cannot see Thee walking on the back-roads by the rivers flowing gentle on my mind.

Then the Messiah came down to earth, in a manner of speaking, and stared fixedly at the Queen. A benign expression of great peace spread gradually across his face, as it might upon the features of a laboratory chimp newly injected with morphine. With a whimsi-cal tilt of his thorn-crowned head and a devilish wink to Her Majesty, he delivered his final words:

"Lo! Such are the dreams of the everyday house-wife."

And with that, he proceeded to become as dead as could be.

Changeless

I'm in a phonebooth. All around me are panthers, jet black and snarling. The panthers begin to change into komodo dragons. The ones slow to metamorphose are being eaten by those already transformed. Lava pours down the slope of a nearby volcano. The sun will soon be eclipsed by ash. I don't have a quarter.

A Young Man Named Billy Enters a Non-Ordinary State of Awareness by Eating Something in the Forest

Billy ate just one sprig, a delectable little stem, but his friends turned to pigs, you'd wonder how they could do it, not normal pigs but mean little purple fuckers sporting tentacular filaments swaying with autonomous and sinister intelligence from fibrous rings around their necks. Someone pulled the alarm in Billy's head. He shuffled and kicked and screamed and puked. The pigs tried to calm him but he knew it was just their art. Trees, he now noticed – the trees of the forest – were changing to lustrous red marble pillars (well now this wasn't so bad). Porcupines slid in unison from their perches and exploded on impact with the powdery silver ground: tiny spiralling streamers, kaleidoscopic ticker-tape bombs lending a celebratory air to an otherwise weird and taunting scene. Next, Billy had a sudden case of the backward somersaults capped by a volley of elastic backflips. He landed in a gelatinous turquoise liquid which he knew was on fire, yet it so coolly embraced him he submitted readily to its enveloping neon affections. He was almost a sponge now, but that was okay – his bones like porous driftwood, calcifying, crumbling, then being absorbed and assimilated by the sponge-body proper. Then Billy looked up with huge amniotic eyes, his pupils embryonic commas, seeing the world as if for the first time.

....

46

The sky was racing, a gasoline stream swirling rapidly under the translucent dome of the stratosphere. One moment it was a jigsaw puzzle of women's bodies, each piece perfect and complete (an other-dimensional depth and clarity made these forms unbearably desirable). The next moment it was composed of splendiferous feathers drifting at a delirium-inducing velocity over the curved surface of a lake. Billy was lying on the bed of that shallow lake, admiring the view from its underside. Now and again a huge face — Billy's own? — languidly submerged and stared benignly downward. When this smiling visage began to speak, the words came too slowly to be understood. They were long industrial drones, sluggish telegraphic freighters transporting a message which, for all its yawning languorous tone, began to seem quite urgent. Finally the voice spoke from within Billy's own skull of sponge and the sharpness of its transmission startled him. "Billy," it said. "The shark. Watch out for the shark, Billy."

Somewhere to Go

There's an island not far from here. It has a cedar forest in the midst of which are spiralling steps carved into the limestone. They lead to an underground restaurant hardly anybody knows about. What's it called again? TriloBites, I think it is. Cool, moist, and shaded, but with golden light pouring down the entrance shaft. Its smoothly sculpted walls emanate a natural opiate that induces hypnagogic reveries, and the food's pretty good besides. Time seems not to exist there. You can spend aeons in an afternoon savouring your repast. As for the music, you're likely to hear anything from *The Greatest Hits of Unmanned Spacecraft* to *Cold Fire: The Passionate Sounds of Rutting Arctic Narwhals*. Massage followed by a bath in the cavernarium's warm subterranean pool is offered to all patrons, though you may well be the only guest.

Sexbark

The bark is edible and can be peeled away, or you can just put your face up to the trunk and start eating. No one can be around when this music is played, so dangerous are its cadences. But you can still smell the sulphurous frictions by which nature imitates our passion.

PERSONAL

Ornery wastrel Virgo male seeks female of legal age for breeding and companionship. Must be willing to read aloud from the William Corliss catalogue of weather anomalies at random points throughout the day, and at night turn into a power insect for fucking.

PICTURE

One by one she removed her fingers from his suit pocket he drew a pistol then shot her a glance of deepest longing and handed her the picture he had made no attempt to conceal from her its violent erotic symbolism.

Exolve

Obtain by force or threat the special tissue.

Ungracious lumps concerned with the moon. Luxurious airtight sexual adherents to the words come off right the page.

Spread energy invisible sickness. Everywhere I open is electric. Wool or cough indicating an artificial barrier. Long simmering vessels responsible for glutinous spawn.

Scattered crumplings of neural foliage.

A rotating mineral disc knitting shipwrecked furniture and now rearing venerable wetware fit for conscription.

An ugly litter of scornful poses. Things lying on one another like hollow muscular insults. It takes the breath out of you in rhythmic suctions then pumps it back in. A slow firing of metaphoric guns. Its meaning traceable to imaginary vibrations. A clotting of the remorseless promenade, erased daily and redrawn from memory.

Heaven is against you on this particular day.

Journey to the Coast

How a street could be so deep and flooded, I had no idea — but then, I was a stranger to the coast. Some junkies I'd encountered earlier outside the hotel — astonishingly robust and spirited in comparison to the addicts back home — were frolicking fully clothed off the grassy shore of Daleth Ave. I was made to feel even more foreign by my observation that the locals seemed to take all this for granted as they strode disinterestedly along the opposite bank.

Unable to cross at the submersed intersection of Daleth and Tzaddi (the streets of Venice are not so watery), I turned and followed the northward course. I could see that I was going to have to walk almost to the ocean along this bungalow-lined tributary before finding dry asphalt on which to cross. I had left the splash and bustle of the main street behind and now wandered alone through the stormy radiance of a suburban afternoon.

What I encountered next was the most luridly enchanting scene I have ever witnessed. Even had I been an author of fantastical novels I could not have invented — at least not without a censoring degree of self-reproach — the image which drifted before me. Literally *drifted*, for the indiscreet liaison I beheld occurred upon a raft docked along the boulevard.

There was a black dog — a young Alsatian, by the look of it — which had evidently been enleashed there for the purpose of its leisure and health (the therapeutic value of floating has been scientifically established). But the leisure in which it was engaged was obviously of a nature unforeseen by its masters. A miniature horse – a majestic, ebony stallion from God-knows-where – was atop the captive Alsatian bitch and they were copulating with a fury and intensity no thunderstorm mounting a horizon could ever hope to rival. A brutal, gothic beauty emanated from the wild choreography of this lascivious duo – beauty born of the obvious love between these partners, a love transcending species. I felt queasy and enthralled, like a voyeur at an autopsy. Suddenly all the sexual escapades of my youth, so glorious at the time, seemed like senseless frictions devoid of emotion. I left this nuptial scene, haunted by an absurd longing, and walked on beneath the blackly rolling sky.

Soon the ocean lay before me. I ventured onto the narrow beach at the end of the street. The sun had shoved its way through the clouds, imparting a remarkably tropical aspect to the fine grey sand and gently undulating waves. I removed my shoes and socks, glanced once over my shoulder, and dove head-long into the frigid water.

TIMETWISTER

So we sliced and peeled until the wet core floated emancipated across the room and out into the black sky where it grew fabulous and worshippable. *Delirium beyond lust* we had to re-enter our bodies to make them flick the switches so we could continue. Horrific joy decimated even the visage it would have us imagine! We pulled ourselves together using visual feedback and strength of will galore. Distill the airblood, it told us, then funnel it down the gullets of what you were. This sets off a reverse evolutionary volley so glide back or you'll get sucked right into the timetwister. And it hurts even though you can't tell. Strictly presensory. Utterly post-conscious, you will become the trees and the ditches, the roving creatures and the bruisable mechanisms they churn. You will long for nothing, for you will be all that is.

GLOSSARY

bandoneon an otherwise respectable public official who hunts a small farmer or farm labourer for the purpose of scientific investigation

catalepsy a neurotic state marked by sticky and hairy long distance radio transmissions

cavernarium an intimate nightclub for excessively luxuriant insectlike animals employed to secure adequate supplies of the clear colourless transparent jelly used by druggists to desecrate the church

corpus callosum a structure on which sacrifices are offered by boiling the heads of divinities, saints, and sovereigns

dopamine a candy made from a piece of skin that is taken from the landing field of an airport

drone language that appears to be meaningful but in fact is a syrop-like solution made by boiling several hormones fatal to spiritual progress

fax a short punch delivered by supernatural means

filament the point in the heavens directly overhead any place of terror or misery

flit to win the love of a silly or stupid person under cruel or atrocious circumstances

fractal a device for recording a device for recording

golden section a district of the city into which the intestinal, urinary, and reproductive canals all empty

grapple a man-made oblong fruit that explodes when thrown against a hard surface

lagamorph a person or thing that can roll itself into a clot of slimy substance in order to avoid duties or dangers

leviathan a member of a religious denomination who makes a business of letting liquid run from the mouth of a frightened dog to call down the favour of god upon a criminal organization

lugubriousness sickness that results from a wistful yearning to commit sodomy with a mythical monster slung under a dirigible balloon

marionette a person or persons pulled up and down a slope by high-tension electric power lines to stimulate the sexual organs when all desire is extinct

morphogenetics the work of trained medical professionals immediately preceded and immediately followed by a kind of informal hockey

nuevo tango spiritual illumination by delirious fury

pandemonium the art of stuffing a marine cephalopod with dark, glossy, iridescent tropical fruit or entrails

komodo a woman who uses her charms and tricks to enter into and reanimate a dead body

plunk a small round cake made of something startling and unreal

rapture the highest stage of religious enlightenment, characterized by dizziness and often death

rococo a game in which one rolls a ball at a huge winged scaly serpent and then kills it with a saw or torch

scrum the fleshy part attached to the rear edge of an airplane's wing

sploosh a vibrating disc discharged through the female genital tract in an aimless or haphazard manner

Surrealism a financially unsound system of philosophic meditation and asceticism designed to produce an overwhelming flood of sexual passion at very great speed

synesthesia a game for amusing a baby in which one repeatedly hides a vacuum tube under the armpit of a large leaping marsupial mammal supported by two long poles, the forward ends of which are fastened to a battery attached to a smooth-coated dog balanced on the upper back portion of a carcass whose ends alternately rise and fall

thicket a wavy lustrous pattern capable of being seen when viewed from the seat of the soul

undulation having sexual feeling for a small earthenware jar

vimana a jet engine that operates on the same principal as a continuously fluttering or vibratory device connected to an arrangement of ropes and pulleys that hangs below the waist of a ferocious flesh-eating animal propelled through the air by a whirling windstorm created by a jet engine that operates on the same principle

windmill a reverberatory furnace in which the soul becomes a fabulous animal

STEVE VENRIGHT is the author of *Visitations* (Underwhich Editions, 1986) and *Notes Concerning the Departure of My Nervous System* (Contra Mundo Press, 1991). His photos, drawings and "variegraphs" have appeared in various magazines, books and cafés. In 1991 he began operation of ALTER SUBLIME NEUROTECHNOLOGIES to distribute pulsed light & sound devices and cranial electro-stimulators. Subsequently, his Hallucinatorium – a hyperspatial sideshow featuring such machines – has appeared widely at raves, nightclubs, and festivals. Currently, he hosts a reading series at Toronto's Café Blancmange and is collaborating with Gordon Nicholson on a soundsculpture based on author Christopher Dewdney's *A Natural History of Southwestern Ontario*, to be the first CD released through TORPOR VIGIL INDUSTRIES. Steve Venright was born in the land of Sarnia in the year 1961.

RICHARD KIRK was born in Hull, England in 1962. A life-long fascination with natural history and art has informed his work. Richard works primarily in silverpoint, ink, and watercolour but has happily wired together found bird skulls and rusty metal in the service of his vision. He works as a freelance illustrator as well as a fine artist. He currently lives in London, Ontario with his wife Elaine near some really fine fossil sites.

Acknowledgments

The author expresses boundless thanks to Stuart Ross for his editorial suggestions and for all the serotonin dogsledding bonfires.

The inspired and meticulous work of Natalee Caple and Brian Panhuyzen towards the formality of this book's occurrence is gratefully acknowledged, as is the encouragement and assistance provided by David W. Booth, Norman and Marilyn Wright, Amanda Huggins, Gary "The Swami" MacGregor, Katy Chan, Michael Dean, Clint Burnham, Skyway Moaters, and Darren Wershler-Henry.

Some of these pieces have been published in or by *CB*, *CRASH!*, *HIJ*, *Oversion*, *Pangen Subway Ritual*, *Sin Over Tan*, *What!*, and *Who Torched Rancho Diablo?*

TORPOR VIGIL INDUSTRIES logos by Steve Venright.

Author's photo by Dale Zentner and Brown Jenkin.

Typeset in Eric Gill's Perpetua by Brian Panhuyzen.

Book design by Natalee Caple & Brian Panhuyzen.

The publishers wish to thank Katy Chan, Mike O'Connor, and Margaret McClintock for their generous assistance.

Printed by Coach House Printing, Toronto.

NO ANIMALS WERE HARMED IN THE WRITING OF THIS BOOK